D1446625

# Love Letters

*To My Granddaughter*

*From Your
Angel Grandmother*

*With Love*

*A Collection of Inspirational Love Letters
By Dr. Aleq Sini*

Sini, Aleq.

To My Granddaughter, From Your Angel Grandmother With Love.

ISBN: 1448608759
EAN-13: 9781448608751

*These collected short letters are dedicated to all the in the Angel grandmothers who love their granddaughters. And to all the granddaughters that are loved by their Angel grandmothers.*

# *Dearest Granddaughter,*

I AM GRATEFUL TO THE UNIVERSE FOR
THE PRIVILEGE OF YOU BEING BORN TO
ME AND BECOMING YOUR GRANDMOTHER.
YOUR PRESENCE HAS MADE LIFE IN THIS
WONDERFUL WORLD TRULY AMAZING.

UNFORTUNATELY, I AM NOW GONE FROM
THIS BEAUTIFUL PLANET, BUT I STILL *AM*
ALTHOUGH I'M IN ANOTHER DIMENSION.
WHEREVER I AM, WHATEVER I DO, I AM YOUR
ANGEL, ALWAYS SENDING YOU THE MESSAGE
OF LOVE.

YOU MIGHT RECEIVE THIS MESSAGE MANY
TIMES, BY ENJOYING THE SUN, THE COMPANY
OF OTHER PEOPLE, BY FEELING AND SEEING
ALL THE LOVE THAT IS AROUND YOU. I AM
ALWAYS SENDING YOU MESSAGES OF LOVE.

I CAN NOW SEE THAT EVERY SINGLE HUMAN
BEING WOULD BE MUCH HAPPIER IF THEY
COULD HEAR FROM THE HEART.  THE BOOK
YOU HOLD IN YOUR HANDS HAS BEEN SENT
TO YOU BY THE INSPIRATION AND FLOW OF

THE AUTHOR WHICH HEARD MY MESSAGE.
NO WORDS, NO BOOKS, NO MESSAGES CAN
EVER DESCRIBE WHAT I REALLY FEEL FOR
YOU, BUT I HOPE THAT THE MESSAGES WILL
HELP YOU OPEN YOUR HEART.
SOME PARTS OF IT MAY NOT RESONATE
WITH YOU AT THIS TIME BUT THEY MAY
EVENTUALLY. OTHER THOUGHTS OR QUOTES
MAY BE JUST THE RIGHT THING AT THE
RIGHT TIME TO POINT YOU IN THE RIGHT
DIRECTION OR SUPPORT YOU. TAKE WHAT
YOU NEED AND LEAVE THE REST. MY MAIN
MESSAGE TO YOU IS THAT I AM SAFE, LOVED
AND HAPPY WHERE I AM AND YOU ARE
LOVED JUST THE WAY YOU ARE.

PEOPLE ARE MIRED IN A FOG, A FOG CALLED
NEGATIVE PROGRAMMING, OR THE ENDLESS
SEARCH FOR APPROVAL. LET ME HELP
DISSIPATE THAT FOG. LET ME HELP OPEN
YOUR EYES AND SEE THAT, FOR YOU, THERE
IS ONLY LOVE.

GRANDDAUGHTER, PLEASE DO NOT CRY FOR
ME. I AM VERY HAPPY WHERE I AM, I ONLY
WISH TO KNOW YOU ARE HAPPY, THAT YOU
ENJOY YOUR LIFE, AND FEEL THE LOVE HERE
FOR YOU IN THIS GREAT PLANET.

ONE DAY, BUT NOT JUST YET, WE WILL MEET AGAIN. THERE IS A SPECIAL MISSION, A PERFECT PURPOSE YOU ARE IN THIS LIFE. LET ME HELP YOU FIND IT AND MOST OF ALL – PLEASE, HAVE FUN, ENJOY LIFE, FEEL THE LOVE.

GRANDDAUGHTER, I CAN NOW SEE WHAT I COULD NOT SEE BEFORE; WHATEVER YOU HAVE, WHATEVER YOU DO, OR WHATEVER YOU BECOME YOU ARE LOVED. IN FACT YOU *ARE* LOVE. PLEASE ENJOY THAT LOVE, AS LONG AND AS MUCH AS POSSIBLE SQUEEZE ALL THE JOY YOU CAN FROM LIFE.

PLEASE LET ME GO AND ENJOY LIFE AS MUCH AS YOU CAN. PLEASE CREATE A LIFE, WITHOUT ME, JUST THE WAY YOU WANT IT TO BE. HONESTLY ALL I WANT IS FOR YOU TO BE HAPPY. I AM HAPPY WHERE I AM. I ENJOY BEING. PLEASE FIND HAPPINESS IN WHATEVER YOU LOVE DOING AND BEING.

I love you dearly,
Your Angel Grandmother

# MESSAGES OF THE LETTERS

# I

# FEEL MY SUPPORT FOR YOU

What else is love but understanding and
rejoicing in the fact that another person
lives, acts, and experiences otherwise
than we do...?

~ FRIEDRICH NIETZSCHE ~

Dearest Granddaughter,

I support you in your

mission.

Your Angel Grandmother

*Dearest Granddaughter,*

*No matter where I am or where you are; I love you. I have always loved you and I love you forever. No time or distance can change the way I feel about you. My love for you is eternal, it will always be.*

*You can feel my love if you look to the moon. You can hear my love whisper to you as the wind ripples the water. I am with you each time you enjoy the wonder of nature.*

*You can feel my love whenever you need, whenever you choose, no matter where you are. Just think of me and feel my love lifting up your happiness. Let my good feelings for you empower you.*

*I support you,*

*Your Angel Grandmother*

# II

# FORGIVE OTHERS AND YOURSELF

One word frees us of all the weight and
pain of life: That word is love.

~ SOPHOCLES ~

Dearest Granddaughter,

I forgive you for

everything. We both know

there is nothing to forgive.

You have given your best.

Please forgive me.

Your Angel Grandmother

*Dearest Granddaughter,*

*I may not have always been the perfect grandmother, the grandmother you desired. I have only done the best I could, the best I knew how. I ask you to forgive me please granddaughter, for all the ways I may have failed you.*

*I know there were times all the love I have for you in my heart was hidden but please know my love is and always has been there. Despite all my flaws and weaknesses there is great love in my heart for you.*

*Please know that I never intended to hurt or disappoint you. Please forgive me, as I urge you to forgive yourself. Truly, because the universe put us together, you were the perfect granddaughter for me even when I could not see it.*

*Your Angel Grandmother*

# III

# OFFER ONLY LOVE

You can judge a person's character by
the way he treats people who can't help
him or hurt him.

~ ANONYMOUS ~

Dearest Granddaughter,
I am so grateful for your
kindness.

Your Angel Grandmother

*Dearest Granddaughter,*

*You are a wonderful and tremendous person. In truth you are pure love. Please as long as you live, remember this; you are magnificent, just the way you are.*

*Don't let anyone, any experience, or any setback convince you otherwise. You and every single person on this planet are created from pure love.*

*When you offer only love, when you speak only love, you are fulfilling your destiny. Let all your words and actions be a blessing to those around you.*

*Speak only truth, offer only love.*

*I love your kindness,*

*Your Angel Grandmother*

# IV

# FEELINGS CREATE

Great men are they who see that spiritual
is stronger than material force, that
thoughts rule the world.

~ RALPH WALDO EMERSON ~

Dearest Granddaughter,

I am so happy for who

I became thanks to you

in my life.

Your Angel Grandmother

*Dearest Granddaughter,*

*Thoughts and the energy of feelings mixed with matter create our World. Thoughts and words have a special vibration. Feel the difference between saying love or hate, happiness or sadness. Thoughts mixed with strong feelings materialize into what we experience on a day to day basis.*

*You must listen to your heart, think and feel all the best thoughts and feelings so the best is what life offers you in return.*

*Have the best in life by reaching for the best. Just be sure you listen to what your inner voice really wants, not what you're supposed to want, or what others want for you.*

*It is only your truest desires that have the strength to materialize.*

*Thank you for your positive thoughts.*

*Your Angel Grandmother*

V

# ENJOY PEACE

First keep the peace within yourself,
then you can also bring peace to others.

~ THOMAS À KEMPIS ~

*Dearest Granddaughter,*

*I love the peace in you.*

*Your Angel Grandmother*

*Dearest Granddaughter,*

*It is possible to carry inner peace with you no matter where you go or what you do. Peace of mind is yours by focusing on things you are grateful for.*

*When you focus on appreciating the positive experiences that happen every day, what is positive grows. Good happens by allowing the energy of the universe to flow through you rather than getting stuck or snagged on negative thoughts or opinions.*

*Enjoying peace of mind every day gives you the opportunity to lead a phenomenal life.*

*When you are at peace you are so gentle. Enjoy it more often.*

*Your Angel Grandmother*

# VI

## BELIEVE

Believe it can be done. When you believe
something can be done, really believe,
your mind will find the ways to do it.
Believing a solution paves the way
to solution.

~ DAVID JOSEPH SCHWARZ ~

*Dearest Granddaughter,*

*I believe in you.*

*Your Angel Grandmother*

*Dearest Granddaughter,*

*To believe and have faith are the most difficult but wonderful blessings in this life. Belief is one of the ultimate principles of consciousness. Trust, faith, and confidence are all aspects of belief; which is intangible and only an act of the will, the mind, and the heart.*

*To believe in yourself, to believe in what you do and who you really are is the ultimate act of faith.*

*Nature shows us that after rain there is sun and the sky is unusually beautiful. To trust in yourself is to trust in the laws of the universe by which we receive what we ask for.*

*But don't allow your beliefs to stagnate, to become old and outdated, no longer relevant to your World. Be willing to upgrade existing beliefs to merge them with new ones. Granddaughter, always be willing to challenge your own beliefs.*

*But whatever happens granddaughter never, never lose faith.*

*Your Angel Grandmother*

# VII

## LOVE AND APPRECIATE YOURSELF

I have often wondered how it is that
every man loves himself more than all
the rest of men, but yet sets less value on
his own opinions of himself than on the
opinions of others.

~ MARCUS AURELIUS ~

*Dearest Granddaughter,*
*I appreciate all the good*
*that you have done.*

*Your Angel Grandmother*

26

*Dearest Granddaughter,*

*I try to understand how difficult it must be to be a granddaughter. I just want you to know that to me you are beautiful, inside and out. Please open your heart and love. Love your body, love your mind, and love the spirit inside you as I do.*

*I see now how every word said by those who care for me was out of love. Remember that no matter what; you are and have always been a beacon of love for me. Always reach within to bring forth all the love you have you have in your heart. Love is all around you! Love is in you. In fact you are made from love!*

*In the morning and evening when you look at yourself in the mirror please let my love offer you the strength, love, and joy you so richly deserve.*

*Be a message of love and gratitude to the universe.*

*Your Angel Grandmother*

# VIII

# BE PRESENT

Most people, even though they don't
know it, are asleep. They're born asleep,
they live asleep, they marry in their
sleep, they breed children in their sleep,
they die in their sleep without ever
waking up. They never understand the
loveliness and the beauty of this thing
that we call human existence.

~ ANTHONY DE MELLO ~

*Dearest Granddaughter,*

*Seize the day.*

*Your Angel Grandmother*

*Dearest Granddaughter,*

*To be present is to truly enjoy the scent of flowers, to really hear the songs of the birds. Being present means not being stuck in the past, not worrying about the future.*

*To be present just let your eyes take in whatever is all around you and learn to see the beauty no matter what form it takes. Quiet the many thoughts in your head and smile. To be present, to be in the moment, is to fully experience and enjoy the moment.*

*Wake up, see there is beauty all around you. Your life is beautiful, this planet is magnificent. Train your eyes to see the truth. Move beyond what happened yesterday, have no fear of tomorrow. Just seize the day, seize the moment! Enjoy the perfection that is possible in every moment. See the real beauty of living in the moment, in the now. Life is magnificent when you focus on the here and now. Life is a blessing when you are really present.*

*I am grateful for your presence in this life.*

*Your Angel Grandmother*

# IX

# LISTEN TO YOUR INNER VOICE

Seek out that particular mental attribute
which makes you feel most deeply and
vitally alive, along with which comes
the inner voice which says, 'This is the
real me,' and when you have found that
attitude, follow it.

~ JAMES TRUSLOW ADAMS ~

*Dearest Granddaughter,*

*I admire your intuition.*

*Your Angel Grandmother*

*Dearest Granddaughter,*

*When you were a child you learned to be strong and independent, to not simply believe what you hear or read. Independence means weighing everything, using your own inner guidance, your inner voice; your intuition. When you are calm and relaxed this inner voice grows stronger. The more certain your inner voice becomes the more clearly you can hear it.*

*Granddaughter I hope you still honor your inner voice by acting on it's wisdom. When you feel your aim is true, go for it. When you feel something is wrong, don't simply ignore it. Get to the bottom of it.*

*Your inner voice will always guide you toward what is positive. Listen to your inner voice and you will create more of what is positive, feel more positive feelings.*

*Spend time in nature, listening to music or find other ways of being alone with your self. Feel how you are guided and your inner voice will become more and more clear. Listen to the influence of that inner voice.*

*Believe in your intuition it is a gift.*

*Your Angel Grandmother*

# X

# BE STRONG

It is not because things are difficult that
we do not dare; It is because we do not
dare that they are difficult.

~ SENECA ~

*Dearest Granddaughter,*

*I see great strength*

*in you.*

*Your Angel Grandmother*

*Dearest Granddaughter,*

*There will be dark moments when you feel down, where worry and fear are all around you. At those times please remember I am always in your heart, offering all my love.*

*It takes real strength to focus on the bright side of life even when you're struggling to understand, to cope, or to forgive. For truly in life there are only setbacks and obstacles. Setbacks and obstacles only identify another way that did not work.*

*The more you focus on the good and the bright the bigger and stronger that light grows.*

*Because of what I learned in life I know how to be strong. Now let me share that strength with you through love.*

*I am so proud and grateful when you are strong.*

*Your Angel Grandmother*

# XI

# ASK INSPIRING QUESTIONS

Quality questions create a quality life.
Successful people ask better questions,
and as a result, they get better answers.

~ ANTHONY ROBBINS ~

*Dearest Granddaughter,*

*Always ask questions*

*that bring your life*

*into positive focus.*

*Your Angel Grandmother*

*Dearest Granddaughter,*

*The way a question is framed limits the potential answers. If you ask questions like, 'Why does everything bad happen to me?' You will continue to get vague, meaningless answers.*

*To bring better outcomes ask better questions not only of yourself but also of the people around you and of the Universe. Don't ask for things you don't want.*

*Instead its better to ask for the things you do want. Ask about the relationships you do want. Ask for the life you do want. 'I don't know how all my needs are met I only know that they are now and I am fulfilled.'*

*Remember there are always empowering ways of asking for what you want. To receive it, you must first believe it.*

*Thank you for teaching me.*

*Your Angel Grandmother*

# XII

## TAKE FULL RESPONSIBILITY

People are always blaming circumstances
for what they are. I don't believe in
circumstances. The people who get
ahead in this world are people who get
up and look for the circumstances they
want, and if they can't find them, make
them.

~ GEORGE BERNARD SHAW ~

*Dearest Granddaughter,*

*There is greatness in you.*

*Your Angel Grandmother*

*Dearest Granddaughter,*

*When you were a child you learned not to cast blame. When things are over and done with, they cannot change. The weather, the neighbors, the environment, or politics are not responsible for your situation. You are, everyone is. Remember your thoughts combined with your feelings create your reality.*

*When you take full responsibility for your life, you create happiness. Then you are creating the World you really want.*

*If you surrender responsibility for your happiness or misery to others, you give up steering your own ship. The moment you believe you are responsible for your happiness and do something to create it, miracles happen. So take action!*

*Taking responsibility allows you to create what you really want. Just as I can have, be, or do anything I want in life; so can you!*

*Your Angel Grandmother*

# XIII

# BE HEALTHY

To wish to be well is a part of becoming well.

~ SENECA ~

Dearest Granddaughter,
Great energy and health
help us enjoy life more.

Your Angel Grandmother

*Dearest Granddaughter,*

*Recognize that your body is the temple of your soul. Care for it as such. Eat fresh and wholesome foods, let your body move! Let only positive energy and healthy thoughts fill your mind. Let only people with positive, wholesome energy fill your heart.*

*Have fun being alive! Laugh, play, enjoy!*

*The better you treat your body, the better you will feel and the healthier you will be. The better you feel, the more you create and attract positive and rewarding experiences. The more you have positive experiences, the better you will feel.*

*Live healthy in body, healthy in mind, and healthy in spirit.*

*Your Angel Grandmother*

# XIV

## COMMIT TO IMPROVE

The moment you commit and quit
holding back, all sorts of unforeseen
incidents, meetings and material
assistance will rise up to help you.

~ NAPOLEON HILL ~

Dearest Granddaughter,
I enjoy seeing you
continue to grow.

Your Angel Grandmother

*Dearest Granddaughter,*

*When you were small and wanted to give up those who
love you urged you to strive to improve, to keep your
chin up. Always be on the lookout for how to become a
better person, to learn more, to make tomorrow even
better than today.*

*Learning brings improvement, happiness, joy, and even
greater love. See how others make improvements in
their life and ask for their guidance. To improve is to
continue growing. To learn and grow is to honor life.*

*Never give up becoming better and better every passing
day.*

*You are great when you strive for better!*

*Your Angel Grandmother*

# XV

## BE THE CHANGE

You must be the change you wish to see
in the world.

~ MAHATMA GANDHI ~

Dearest Granddaughter,
I love you just the way
you are.

Your Angel Grandmother

*Dearest Granddaughter,*

*Although there are several billion people on this Earth, each and every one is entirely unique.*

*As you strive to improve yourself it is important to recognize that in reality you only compete with yourself. Whenever you seek to change yourself, change your views. You try to best and better who you were yesterday. Today you work to be better, wiser, and happier.*

*Attempting to gain power over others through conflict is not a fruitful investment of energy. Instead bless their success or mistake and learn to think beyond it. Your way will be as unique as you are.*

*Avoid comparing friends or loved ones to others, for, like you, they are also unique. By focusing on their good qualities they will offer more good. Don't try to change your friends, your environment, the people that are around you, but be the change you want to see in them. By changing yourself, by growing, everything and everyone will change.*

*Your Angel Grandmother*

# XVI

# BE PROUD

I know of no more encouraging fact than the
unquestioned ability of a man to elevate his life by
conscious endeavor.

~ HENRY DAVID THOREAU ~

*Dearest Granddaughter,*

*I am proud of you.*

*Your Angel Grandmother*

*Dearest Granddaughter,*

*Whatever you choose to do in life I am proud of you.
From my heart's core, I support you. In whatever you
do, take pride in yourself. Whatever comes your way,
choose to return to happiness again and again.*

*Being a part of this wonderful creation really is an
honor. When you walk through this World as a credit to
yourself you are also a credit to me. Feel satisfaction
from the good things you have done and continue to do.*

*Be gratified by your achievements. Honor who you are
becoming. Recognize your true value in this complex
and miraculous World as I have only begun to do.*

*I am proud of you.*

*Your Angel Grandmother*

# XVII

# LIVE YOUR PASSION

Clarity of mind means clarity of passion, too; this is
why a great and clear mind loves ardently and sees
distinctly what it loves.

~ BLAISE PASCAL ~

Dearest Granddaughter,

Do what you love

and life is play.

Give thanks for the

gift of life.

Your Angel Grandmother

*Dearest Granddaughter,*

*There are some things some tasks, some activities that really light your inner spark. To recognize what those are imagine what you'd be willing to pay to do.*

*Make absolutely sure of what you want in life. Clarity equals power. The more clarity you have the more likely you are to reap the success you deserve. Harness you passion, aim it toward your desires and it will propel you.*

*Everyone has dreams. Those who don't are only afraid to face them. Cast off fear and acknowledge your deep desires. Find your passion and live your dreams. To live who you really are, practice doing the things the way the person you want to be would.*

*When you find your passion, when there is clarity in what you want to be and do, make sure you use all your strength and action to get it. When it comes from you heart, you will get all the support you need, but you must take action.*

*When you live your passion, the World becomes your playground. You are the most important person in your life. Find your own strength, live your own passion, before reaching out to help others.*

*Only a sure swimmer can rescue a drowning man.*

*Your Angel Grandmother*

# XVIII

# CONTRIBUTE

Any person who contributes to
prosperity must prosper in turn.

~ EARL NIGHTINGALE ~

Dearest Granddaughter,

Thank you for teaching others to do good in the World.

Your Angel Grandmother

*Dearest Granddaughter,*

*Growing up you saw all the ordinary ways of showing kindness or respect to others. Perhaps helping someone carry heavy bags, or by giving up a seat on a crowded train. So now ask yourself, 'How do I help make this a better World?'*

*It really feels wonderful to make things more pleasant, more interesting, or simply better for those around you. Ask your inner voice what you can offer others.*

*This creates an energetic connection which benefits both. Giving keeps the positive inspiration flowing in and around. Giving makes you a dynamic element of the universe.*

*Contributions are not only financial but occur any time you offer your time or attention to another.*

*I am so grateful for all the ways you contributed to who I became.*

*Your Angel Grandmother*

# XIX

# BE GRATEFUL

Gratitude is not only the greatest of
virtues, but the parent of all others.

~ CICERO ~

Dearest Granddaughter,
For all that you have done
for me I am grateful to
you forever.

Your Angel Grandmother

*Dearest Granddaughter,*

*Whatever happens, be grateful for the small things in
life. Remember to be grateful for the air you breathe
and the water you drink, for the sun that shines and for
the rain that falls.*

*Be grateful for all the people around you, they are your
students and your teachers. Each experience offers a
new chance, another opportunity to grow and evolve.*

*The precious gift that is being alive deserves a heart
overflowing with gratitude. Like the gratitude I have in
my heart for the granddaughter that you are and have
been.*

*In the morning be grateful for the gift that is life. Feel
gratitude toward the others you meet. At night, feel
gratitude for another magical day of living.*

*I feel deeply grateful for everything that you have done
for me.*

*Thank you,*

*Your Angel Grandmother*

# XX

## BE HONEST

I cannot find language of sufficient
energy to convey my sense of the
sacredness of private integrity.

~ RALPH WALDO EMERSON ~

Dearest Granddaughter,

I appreciate your honesty.

It will stay with me

forever.

Your Angel Grandmother

*Dearest Granddaughter,*

*I can hardly remember all the times as a child you
struggled to stay on the path of honesty. Since then
you've surely been tempted to take shortcuts. But
remember from growing up that it takes courage to stay
honest, that a happy future is an honest future.*

*If you've made mistakes, if you've been dishonest, you
can still change! That telling the truth may have a cost
but the truth will lift you up, get you back on the right
path.*

*When you falter on the path of honesty, pick yourself
up immediately. Don't make excuses or cast blame.
Don't look back. You've learned from the experience.
You are now a different person than you were at the
time of the mistake. Simply, don't do that again. Live in
the present, enjoy your life and be happy about the
future.*

*Remember the words of Dr. John Demartini, 'No matter
what I've done or not done, I'm worthy of Love.'*

*Thank you for showing me honesty in your heart.*

*Your Angel Grandmother*

# XXI

# BE PLAYFUL, CURIOUS

The great man is he who does not lose his child-heart.

~ MENCIUS ~

Dearest Granddaughter,
Thank you for reminding
me what it means to be
playful.

Your Angel Grandmother

*Dearest Granddaughter,*

*The laughing playing, fun child that you once were, is still in you. Remember that child again, be that child again enjoying who you really are.*

*Set your curiosity loose, follow your truth and follow your passion with the freedom and determination of a child. Following your own path will bring you what you want most deeply.*

*Like the child who plays, having fun, enjoy your life. Spend time doing things that entertain that child in you. Do even the things you must do with humor and a little bit of silliness.*

*Your life really is a playground. Run in the grass, sing in the rain, or wear fancy dress for no reason. Just laugh and have fun.*

*You shine, when you are playful.*

*Your Angel Grandmother*

# XXII

# SEEK THOSE WHO INSPIRE

Associate with men of good quality if
you esteem your own reputation; for it is
better to be alone than in bad company.

~ GEORGE WASHINGTON ~

*Dearest Granddaughter,*

*You are my inspiration.*

*Your Angel Grandmother*

*Dearest Granddaughter,*

*Look to others for inspiration. Seek those who can draw you closer to where you want to be. Being in the company of those you admire and strive to be like is a delight. Choose wisely, who to turn to for inspiration.*

*Because you gain or lose energy in relationships you must select the company you keep with care. Observe how you feel in the presence of certain people. Then make choices according to your own well being, your own best interest, first.*

*Reading books and biographies and listening to the stories of others is helpful. Be especially curious about people who have achieved what you feel is 'great.' They have left a trail to follow.*

*Granddaughter let me be your angel.*

*Your Angel Grandmother*

# XXIII

## FEEL GOOD

There are only two ways to live your life.
One is as though nothing is a miracle.
The other is as if everything is.

~ ALBERT EINSTEIN ~

Dearest Granddaughter,

Whatever you do,

wherever you are,

remember to enjoy,

feel good and be happy.

Your Angel Grandmother

*Dearest Granddaughter,*

*Feeling good is always better than feeling bad. In fact simply feeling good may be one of the most important things we can do in life.*

*It is not only possible to be playful, be happy, and enjoy life, it is desirable! Whatever your circumstances joy, love, happiness and gratitude come from your inner being.*

*Every good thought, every positive feeling adds to the balance of the whole World. Your joy could tip the scales and bring the entire planet into a joyful new state of being.*

*Your joy is contagious, let it spread.*

*Your Angel Grandmother*

# My Dearest Granddaughter,

I LOVE YOU, I WILL ALWAYS LOVE YOU! AS
LONG YOU ARE ON THIS PLANET REMEMBER,
THAT WHEREVER YOU GO, WHENEVER YOU
FEEL SAD, ANGRY OR FEARFUL, REMEMBER
THAT MY LOVE IS HERE TO COMFORT YOU. I
LOVE YOU DEEPLY.


Truly yours,
Angel Grandmother

You can place my photo here or you can write your favorite quote or any thoughts that you might want to share with me!

My Dearest Granddaughter,

Whenever you want – write to me, write to me about your doubts or fears, ask me for guidance and I will find other angels working on planet Earth, or find TV shows, books, teachers, or magic 'coincidences' that will help you on your way to where you want to go, or to become who you want to be. Please understand that along the way you may not understand every single step, but keep the faith, believe and expect and you will receive my messages for sure. In the end you will always receive what you will truly ask for from your heart!

Your Angel Grandmother


Write to me

.................................................................................................................

.................................................................................................................

.................................................................................................................

.................................................................................................................

.................................................................................................................

.................................................................................................................

.................................................................................................................

.................................................................................................................

.................................................................................................................

.................................................................................................................

.................................................................................................................

.................................................................................................................

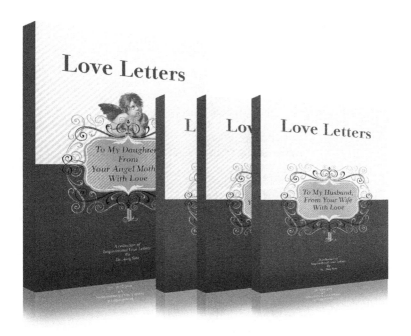

The 'LOVE LETTERS' BOOK SERIES
has tailored these core messages of the heart
into intimate conversations between loved
ones. Please note that all the books carry the
same core message with a slightly different
tone. You can pass these thoughts and feelings
on to *your* loved ones by purchasing one of our
additional titles.

BOOKS     www.aleqsini.com

- ☐ 1. To My Mother, From Your Son With Love
- ☐ 2. To My Father, From Your Son With Love
- ☐ 3. To My Father, From Your Daughter With Love
- ☐ 4. To My Mother from Your Daughter With Love
- ☐ 5. To My Son, From Your Mother With Love
- ☐ 6. To My Son, From Your Father With Love
- ☐ 7. To My Daughter, From Your Mother With Love
- ☐ 8. To My Daughter, From Your Father With Love
- ☐ 9. To My Grandfather, From Your Grandson With Love
- ☐ 10. To My Grandfather, From Your Granddaughter With Love
- ☐ 11. To My Grandmother, from Your Grandson With Love
- ☐ 12. To My Grandmother, From Your Granddaughter With Love
- ☐ 13. To My Grandson, From Your Grandfather With Love
- ☐ 14. To My Grandson, From Your Grandmother With Love
- ☐ 15. To My Granddaughter, From Your Grandmother With Love
- ☐ 16. To My Granddaughter, From Your Grandfather With Love
- ☐ 17. To My Wife, From Your Husband With Love
- ☐ 18. To My Husband, From Your Wife With Love
- ☐ 19. To My Girlfriend, From Your Boyfriend With Love
- ☐ 20. To My Boyfriend, From Your Girlfriend With Love
- ☐ 21. To My Uncle, From Your Nephew With Love
- ☐ 22. To My Aunt, From Your Nephew With Love
- ☐ 23. To My Aunt, From Your Niece With Love
- ☐ 24. To My Uncle, From Your Niece With Love
- ☐ 25. To My Cousin, From Your Cousin With Love
- ☐ 26. To My Best Friend, From Your Friend With Love
- ☐ 27. To My Mentor, From Your Student With Gratitude
- ☐ 28. To My Teacher, From Your Student With Gratitude
- ☐ 29. To My Father, From Your Angel Son With Love
- ☐ 30. To My Mother, From Your Angel Son With Love

☐    31.   To My Father, From Your Angel Daughter With Love

☐    32.   To My Mother, From Your Angel Daughter With Love

☐    33.   To My Son, From Your Angel Mother With Love

☐    34.   To My Son, From Your Angel Father With Love

☐    35.   To My Daughter, From Your Angel Father With Love

☐    36.   To My Daughter, From Your Angel Mother With Love

☐    37.   To My Grandfather, From Your Angel Grandson With Love

☐    38.   To My Grandfather, From Your Angel Granddaughter With Love

☐    39.   To My Grandmother, From Your Angel Granddaughter With Love

☐    40.   To My Grandmother, From Your Angel Grandson With Love

☐    41.   To My Grandson, From Your Angel Grandmother With Love

✓    42.   To My Granddaughter, From Your Angel Grandmother With Love

☐    43.   To My Granddaughter, From Your Angel Grandfather With Love

☐    44.   To My Grandson, From Your Angel Grandfather With Love

☐    45.   To My Wife, From Your Angel Husband With Love

☐    46.   To My Husband, From Your Angel Wife With Love

☐    47.   To My Boyfriend, From Your Angel Girlfriend With Love

☐    48.   To My Girlfriend, From Your Angel Boyfriend With Love

☐    49.   To My Best Friend, From Your Angel Dog With Love

☐    50.   To My Best Friend, From Your Angel Cat With Love

☐    51.   To My Student, From Your Teacher With Gratitude

☐    52.   To My Student, From Your Mentor With Gratitude

☐    53.   To My Daughter, From Your Angel Soldier Father With Love

☐    54.   To My Son, From Your Angel Soldier Father With Love

☐    55.   To My Daughter, From Your Angel Soldier Mother With Love

☐    56.   To My Son, From Your Angel Soldier Mother With Love

...

Please help us draw more love out of our hearts.
Please help us all to see that we are truly one, that
there are no borders, no differences among us. We
belong to the same universe. Let us all offer more
love to the World.
Visit our website to share your story about how giving
this book improved your relationship or how sharing
your deeper thoughts with another via this book has
helped you.

## www.aleqsini.com/sharestory

Made in United States
North Haven, CT
23 April 2022

18491151R00065